Celebrate
Rosh Hashanah
& Yom Kippur

Deborah Heiligman
Consultant, Rabbi Shira Stern

NATIONAL GEOGRAPHIC
WASHINGTON, D.C.

These girls in Kirkland, Washington, enjoy apples and honey on Rosh Hashanah.

honey

Every September or October Jewish people all over the world celebrate Rosh Hashanah and Yom Kippur. We celebrate with honey, prayers, and the shofar.

prayers

We also observe these holidays by looking at the year that has just past. We look inside ourselves to see how we can be better people. We ask God for help. These holidays are also called the Days of Awe and the High Holy Days.

v *A shofar*

We look forward to new beginnings. We are in awe of God's power.

shofar

We celebrate Rosh Hashanah

first. "Rosh" is a Hebrew word that means "head." "Shanah" means "year." So Rosh Hashanah means head of the year—or New Year. We believe that God created the world at this time more than 5,000 years ago.

> *Jewish New Year's greeting cards*

We are filled with hope.

< *Rabbi Ambros Makuwaza, back left, leads his congregation in song and dance during a Rosh Hashanah service in Rusape, Zimbabwe.*

We send New Year's cards to friends and family. We say, "May your year be filled with sweetness, may your year be filled with good health, may your year be filled with *shalom,* peace." As the new year begins, we are filled with hope for a good year.

∧ A high holy day challah

Like all Jewish holidays,
Rosh Hashanah begins at sundown.
We light candles and say a prayer.

We light candles and say a prayer.

< A woman in Bangkok, Thailand, says the blessing over the candles before Rosh Hashanah services.

We sit down with our families for a delicious holiday dinner. We eat a special bread called challah. On Rosh Hashanah our challah is round to show that life is a circle from birth to death to birth again.

> A boy in Israel helps his mother make challah for Rosh Hashanah. They add raisins and coat the bread with cinnamon-sugar for a sweet New Year.

< In Palm Beach, California, Rabbi Moshe Scheiner and his children light candles for the beginning of Rosh Hashanah.

7

Jewish people from different countries eat different foods at Rosh Hashanah. Some of us eat foods that come from the head of an animal, such as tongue. Others eat fish heads.

∧ *Honey for a sweet year*

We eat honey for a sweet year.

Some of us eat pomegranates, because it is said that a pomegranate has 613 seeds. There are 613 commandments, or things we must do, in the Torah, our holy book.

But the most important food is honey. We all eat honey for a sweet year. We dip our challah in honey; we dip apples in honey.

∧ *Girls in Israel share a platter of pomegranates during Rosh Hashanah.*

< *A chef in Jerusalem, Israel, prepares what he calls the "biggest gefilte fish." Gefilte fish is made of a variety of fish ground up.*

On Rosh Hashanah we go to synagogue to pray. We go in the evening and during the day. We listen to the blowing of a special ram's horn called the shofar. The sound of the shofar wakes us up and calls us to prayer. We hear: *Teki'ah! Shva'rim! Tru'ah!*

The shofar calls us to prayer.

The shofar is not easy to blow. It takes special skill. The shofar is blown 100 times each day of Rosh Hashanah!

> Rabbi Xai demonstrates how to blow a shofar in his synagogue in Porto, Portugal.

We pray for a good year.

We sing special prayers, some out loud, some silently, and we think about the year ahead. We ask God to help us live another year, to inscribe us in the Book of Life.

∨ *These Jews in a synagogue in Morocco are bringing out the Torah. Part of the service on Rosh Hashanah is reading from the Torah.*

We sing

special prayers.

∧ A father in Jerusalem, Israel, reads from a prayer book with his children.

We also read from the Torah.

After services we greet our friends by saying, *"L'shanah tova teekataivu. May you be inscribed for a good year."*

Thousands of Jews stand around a lake
in Uman, Ukraine, for a Tashlikh service.

We cast away
our sins.

On the first day of Rosh Hashanah,

in the afternoon, we have a special service to cast away our sins. It is called *Tashlikh,* which means to send away.

We try to go to a river, or another body of water. We turn our pockets inside out, as if emptying out all our sins. Or we throw pieces of bread into the water—the pieces of bread represent our sins.

We think about
how we can be
better people.

During the ten days that

start with Rosh Hashanah and end with Yom Kippur, we think about all we have done throughout the year. These ten days are called the Days of Repentance. We think about how we can be better people, better Jews. We ask our friends and family to forgive us for all we have done wrong. And we forgive them.

It is a time when we think of others. We think of those who are needy. We give *tzedakah,* or charity.

< *At a monument for fallen soldiers, an Israeli soldier remembers the dead during the Days of Repentance.*

Yom Kippur is a very holy day.

Adults and teenagers fast. Children over nine try to eat less than usual. This is to place more importance on prayer than on our physical needs.

Yom Kippur is a very holy day.

On *Erev* Yom Kippur, the evening of Yom Kippur, we eat a good but light meal before the sun goes down. We make sure to have challah and apples and honey again. Adults and teenagers will not eat or drink anything for the next 25 hours.

> An immigrant to Israel from India follows tradition by blessing his son at sundown on Erev Yom Kippur.

We hope we can be better.

> *Rabbi Beth Singer, right, and Cantor Wendy Marcus, of Temple Beth Am, in Seattle, Washington, are dressed in white for Yom Kippur services.*

< People say prayers at the ancient holy site known as the Western Wall in Jerusalem, Israel, on Erev Yom Kippur.

∧ Cover of a 1908 musical arrangement of Kol Nidre.

We go to synagogue on

Erev Yom Kippur. Some of us dress all in white, to symbolize purity. Some of us do not wear gold jewelry or leather. This is to show that we are worshipping God, not things.

We hear the chanting of an ancient prayer called Kol Nidre. It means "All Vows." As we listen to the beautiful melody, we think about the vows we will make, promises to be better. We hope we can be better.

Yom Kippur is a day to really think about all we have done wrong. We list all the wrongs we have committed during the year. Some of us pound our fists into our chests. We say our sins out loud together as a community. We have sinned. We have done wrong. Forgive us!

It is a day to begin again.

We ask God for forgiveness. We forgive ourselves. We atone, or make up, for the wrongs we have done.

It is a day to begin again. Yom Kippur is a solemn time, but it is not sad. We are happy to be with our family. We are happy to be with God.

< This man in Mexico pounds his chest with his fist as he prays during the week between Rosh Hashanah and Yom Kippur.

23

We are ready to

At the end of Yom Kippur

we hear one long note on the shofar: *teki'ah gedolah.*

We feel good from a long day of praying.

We gather together with family and friends. We eat a meal to break the fast. We laugh. We are ready to start a new year. Happy New Year!

< A boy practices blowing the shofar under a pomegranate tree in Israel.

start a new year.

MORE ABOUT ROSH HASHANAH & YOM KIPPUR

Contents

Just the Facts

WHO CELEBRATES IT: Jews

WHAT: Rosh Hashanah is the Jewish New Year and Yom Kippur is the Day of Atonement. After the Sabbath, they are the two holiest days.

ALSO KNOWN AS: The High Holy Days, the High Holidays, and the Days of Awe.

WHEN: In September or October. Since the dates are based on the Hebrew calendar they are not on the same days every year. Rosh Hashanah begins at sundown before the Hebrew month Tishrei begins. Yom Kippur is on the tenth day of Tishrei.

HOW LONG: Rosh Hashanah is celebrated for two days by many people. Some Jews observe it for one day. Yom Kippur is one day. Like all Jewish holidays they begin and end at sundown.

RITUALS: Prayer, fasting, blowing the shofar.

FOOD: Food with honey, apples dipped in honey, challah, pomegranates, fish heads.

Al Het

During the Yom Kippur service we confess our sins and ask for forgiveness. Here is a brief adaptation of the *Al Het* prayer. Al Het means "for the sin." Notice the prayer is said as a "we"—that is to show that we are part of a community.

For the wrong that we have done before you in the closing of our heart,
And for the wrong that we have done without knowing what we do,
For the wrong that we have done before on purpose or by mistake,
And for the wrong that we have done before you by being violent,
For the wrong that we have done before you through foolishness of speech,
And for the wrong that we have done before you through greed,
For the wrong that we have done before you by giving someone a mean look,
And for the wrong we have done before you by being mean.
For the wrong that we have done before you by lying to a friend,
and for the wrong that we have done before you by unwillingness to change.
For the wrong that we have done before you by hating.
For all these wrongs, please forgive us, pardon us, help us atone!

The Torah

The Torah is the holy book of the Jewish people. It is also known as The Five Books of Moses because it is made up of the first five books of the Bible: Genesis, Exodus, Leviticus, Numbers, and Deuteronomy. The Torah is special because the words are hand-lettered in Hebrew on a scroll. Only certain people, called scribes, can make a Torah. It takes a very special skill and learning. It also takes special skill and learning to read the Torah. The Hebrew is written without vowels, unlike the Hebrew in a prayer book. It is read by chanting, or singing, the words. People who can chant from the Torah are often invited to do so

^ A close look at a Torah

at Rosh Hashanah and Yom Kippur services. Many children learn how to do this when they become a bar or bat mitzvah when they are 13 (or for some girls, 12).

The Shofar

^ A Jew in Peru blows his shofar.

The shofar is an ancient instrument. It is mentioned in the Bible many times. It is made from the horn of a ram. The shofar is difficult to blow, and the people who blow it at Rosh Hashanah and Yom Kippur services are very much appreciated and honored. Three different notes are blown: an unbroken sound, called *teki'ah*; a wailing sound broken into three parts, called *shva'rim*; and a kind of tooting sound broken into nine parts, called *tru'ah*.

The sound of the shofar is like an alarm clock, or a wake-up call. It says, "Really wake up now, think about your life, think about the past year, pray well, pay attention!"

Rabbi Shira's Honey Cake

This delicious honey cake is light and airy because of the egg whites.

INGREDIENTS:
5 eggs
¾ cup brown sugar
¼ cup oil
¾ cup honey
2 teaspoons cinnamon
½ teaspoon nutmeg
½ teaspoon vanilla
1 ¾ cups self-rising flour

YOU WILL ALSO NEED:
An electric mixer to beat the egg whites
A whisk
A wooden spoon
A 10-inch cake pan sprayed with vegetable
 oil and then lightly dusted with flour
Confectioner's sugar
Slivered almonds, lightly toasted (optional)
An adult to help you

1. Preheat oven to 350°F.

2. Separate egg whites and egg yolks.

3. Beat egg whites with a mixer until they look stiff.

4. Slowly add sugar to egg whites with mixer at lowest speed.

5. Add egg yolks and oil to egg-white mixture with a whisk. Be gentle. Keep stirring.

6. Add honey, cinnamon, nutmeg, vanilla, and flour using a wooden spoon. Remember to be gentle. Stir until all the flour is absorbed.

7. Pour batter into prepared pan.

8. Bake at 350°F for 45 minutes.

9. Check for doneness by inserting a toothpick into the center of the cake. If it comes out gooey, the cake's not done yet. Try not to open the door of the oven until you think the time is up.

10. Cool in pan for 15 minutes. Loosen the edges and bottom of the cake with a long knife. Turn the cake onto a rack.

11. Once the cake is completely cool, place it on a plate. To make it look pretty, shake confectioner's sugar on top. Sprinkle with the almonds if you like.

Find Out More

BOOKS

Those with a star (*) are especially good for children.

*Bogot, Howard I., Robert Orkand, and Joyce Orkand. *Gates of Awe: Holy Day Prayers for Young Children.* Central Conference of American Rabbis, 1991. This book, published by the Reform Movement of Judaism, is very good for young children.

*Fishman, Cathy Goldberg. *On Rosh Hashanah and Yom Kippur.* Atheneum, 1997. A nice book with pretty illustrations.

Prayer Book for the Days of Awe. The Reconstructionist Press, 1999. This is the prayer book I used for reference; there are others published by different movements in Judaism.

Telushkin, Joseph. *Jewish Literacy.* William Morrow, 1991. The subtitle of this book is: *The Most Important Things to Know About the Jewish Religion, Its People and Its History.* I agree.

EDUCATIONAL EXTENSIONS

1. Honey, challah, and the shofar are all symbols of Rosh Hashanah and Yom Kippur. Pick one of these items and explain why it is important, including what it represents and how it is used.

2. Rosh Hashanah and Yom Kippur take place over ten days. Can you describe some of the traditions that occur on one of these days and explain why they take place?

3. Pick a favorite photograph from the text and reread its caption. What symbols of Rosh Hashanah and Yom Kippur can you see in the photo? (Hint: Expand upon the information given and the visual details in relation to the context of the page.)

4. Write an informative/explanatory essay on the Days of Repentance and how they relate to the Jewish New Year. Explain how these days are celebrated, and what they represent about both the past and coming year.

5. Present your explanatory essay to your class, friends, or parents. Explain what you discovered, what facts interested you most, and the sources you used.

< *A girl in Los Angeles, California, practices blowing the shofar.*

Glossary

Atone (Uh-TONE): To make up for. If you do something bad you atone, or make up for it.

Cast away: Get rid of.

Charity: Money or help that is given to people in need. Jews use the Hebrew word *tzedakah* (tzeh-DAH-kah), which means "justice." When you give tzedakah, you are making things just.

Erev (AIR-ev): The eve of a holiday. Since all Jewish holidays begin at sundown, the Erev is when the holiday begins.

Fast: Go without food and drink.

Sabbath: A day of rest and religious time every week, beginning on Friday at sundown and ending Saturday night.

Shofar (SHOW-far): A musical instrument made out of a ram's horn.

Sin: Bad behavior that goes against religious or moral laws.

Synagogue (Sin-uh-GOG): A Jewish place of worship. Also called a temple or a shul.

Torah (Toe-RAH): The Jewish holy book, consisting of the first five books of the Bible.

Where This Book's Photos Were Taken

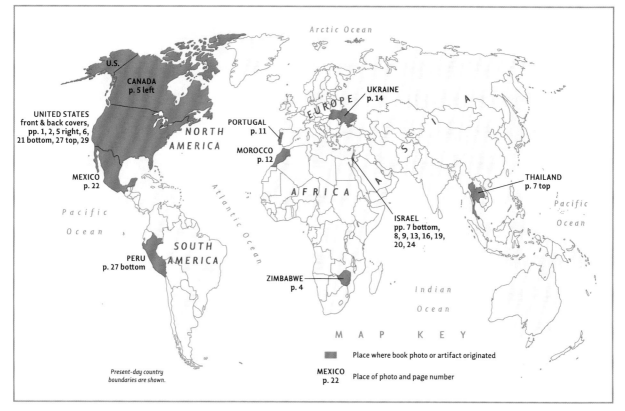

U.S.

CANADA
p. 5 left

UNITED STATES
front & back covers,
pp. 1, 2, 5 right, 6,
21 bottom, 27 top, 29

NORTH
AMERICA

Arctic Ocean

UKRAINE
p. 14

EUROPE

PORTUGAL
p. 11

MOROCCO
p. 12

AFRICA

THAILAND
p. 7 top

A S I A

MEXICO
p. 22

Pacific

Ocean

Atlantic Ocean

ISRAEL
pp. 7 bottom,
8, 9, 13, 16, 19,
20, 24

Pacific

Ocean

SOUTH
AMERICA

PERU
p. 27 bottom

ZIMBABWE
p. 4

Indian

Ocean

M A P   K E Y

Place where book photo or artifact originated

MEXICO
p. 22

Place of photo and page number

*Present-day country
boundaries are shown.*

Rosh Hashanah and Yom Kippur: Coming Full Circle

by Rabbi Shira Stern

Days of wonder, days of awe, days of introspection. The High Holidays actually begin with a month of preparation—called "Elul"—as we evaluate how the last year has gone and what we want to change to make the next year better. The word "Elul" is an acrostic for the Hebrew phrase, "Ani L'dodi, V'dodi Li"— "I am my beloved's and my beloved is mine." This is a metaphor for our relationship with God. But it's not about a romantic relationship; it's a bond between parent and child. Especially for the youngest children, God "the parent" is a natural concept. We want to feel so close to God that God will forgive us for the wrongs we have done. To inspire ourselves, we mark each day by blowing the shofar and include special prayers that begin the repenting process.

While Rosh Hashanah celebrates Creation, the real work gets done during the intervening days before Yom Kippur, the holiest fast day of the year. Before we can stand in front of God to be absolved, we must approach everyone we have hurt, or who has hurt us, to ask for and to grant forgiveness. It is not enough to say, "I'm sorry," with the intention of sinning again in the future; we must be willing to change for real. A Hassidic tale reminds us that our words have power: A young boy is shunned by his best friend because he once revealed a secret that became the gossip topic of the school yard. Apologizing didn't help, so his rabbi instructed him to take his pillow, climb the watch tower, and empty his pillow into the wind. When the boy returned to his rabbi, he was then gently instructed to gather up all the errant feathers. "But that's impossible!" he said. "They're scattered everywhere." The rabbi replied, "That's what happens with words we use to hurt others: It's impossible to take them all back. But we can try not to do the same thing again."

The shofar is the central High Holiday image. It comes from the story of the binding of Isaac. Before Abraham can harm his son, God provides a ram to replace the boy on the altar. The ram's horn is blown on both days of Rosh Hashanah and signals the end of Yom Kippur. It is not generally played on the Sabbath, in keeping with the traditional restriction on using instruments that day.

The most solemn and awe-filled service is Kol Nidrei, which ushers in Yom Kippur eve. It means "all vows" and refers to the promises we are about to make. If we do our best but cannot fulfill them all, we ask God to understand. The fast lasts 25 hours, from sundown to an hour after sundown the next day. Some wear a white kittel—a special white robe. In a service called Yizkor, we think about loved ones who have died, and we light memorial candles in small glass jars that burn for all of Yom Kippur.

We celebrate again just five days later with the holiday of Sukkot, when we are commanded by God to build a temporary hut (called a sukkah) where we will eat all our meals for a week. We invite guests, thank God for a successful harvest, and pray for rain to water the crops for the coming year. At the end of Sukkot, we mark the conclusion of the High Holiday season with the holiday of Simkhat Torah. This is the celebration of Torah, when we read the last few lines of the scroll, then immediately begin again with the first words of Genesis.

We have come full circle in the Jewish year, and we are spiritually ready to begin again.

Rabbi Shira Stern is a pastoral counselor and chaplain in Marlboro, N.J., and director of the Center for Pastoral Care and Counseling.

For Rabbi Shira Stern, with thanks and love

PICTURE CREDITS

Front cover, Geoff Manasse/Getty Images; Back cover, Michael Newman/Photo Edit Inc.; Spine, Lynn Watson/Shutterstock; 1, Jim Evans/Jackson Hole News/Associated Press; 2, Geoff Manasse/IPN Stock; 3, Yehoshua Halevi/Golden Light Images; 4 (UP), The Jewish Museum/Art Resource, NY; 4 (LO), The Jewish Museum/Art Resource, NY; 5, Denis Farrell/Associated Press; 6 (UP), C. Kurt Holter/Shutterstock; 6 (LO), Greg Lovett/Palm Beach Post/ZUMA Press; 7 (UP), Ouriel Allouche/Chabad-Lubavitch; 7 (LO), Yehoshua Halevi/Golden Light Images; 8 (UP), Francois Etienne du Plessis/Shutterstock; 8 (LO), Pierre Terdjman/Flash 90; 9, Nati Shohat/Flash 90; 10-11, Nuno Guimaraes/WPN; 12, Abdelhak Senna/AFP/Getty Images; 13, Nati Shohat/Flash 90; 14-15, Gil Cohen Magen/Reuters; 16-17, Pool photo/SIPA; 19, Yehoshua Halevi/Golden Light Images; 20, Flash90; 21 (UP), The Image Works; 21 (LO), Geoff Manasse/IPN Stock; 22, Bryan Schwartz; 24-25, Yehoshua Halevi/Golden Light Images; 27 (UP), Rogelio Solis/Associated Press; 27 (LO), Bryan Schwartz; 28, Brad Hoffman; 29, Michael Newman/Photo Edit Inc.

STAFF FOR THIS BOOK

Nancy Laties Feresten, *Vice President, Editor-in-Chief of Children's Books*
Bea Jackson, *Design and Illustrations Director, Children's Books*
Amy Shields, *Executive Editor, Children's Books*
Marfé Ferguson Delano, *Project Editor*
Lori Epstein, *Illustrations Editor*
Melissa Brown, *Project Designer*
Callie Broaddus, *Associate Designer*
Carl Mehler, *Director of Maps*
Priyanka Lamichhane, *Assistant Editor*
Rebecca Baines, *Editorial Assistant*
Paige Towler, *Editorial Assistant*
Jennifer A. Thornton, *Managing Editor*
Gary Colbert, *Production Director*
Lewis R. Bassford, *Production Manager*
Maryclare Tracy, Nicole Elliott, *Manufacturing Managers*
Kelsey Carlson, *Education Consultant*

Front cover: Assisted by his father, a boy in Seattle, Washington, tries to coax sound from a large shofar.
Back cover: A sister and brother in Los Angeles, California, dip apple slices into honey as part of their Rosh Hashanah celebration.
Title page: Larry Thal blows his shofar from his backyard in Jackson Hole, Wyoming. He is wearing a prayer shawl called a talis.

Published by National Geographic Partners, LLC.

Text copyright © 2007 Deborah Heiligman
Compilation copyright © 2007 National Geographic Society
Reprinted in paperback and library binding, 2016

Since 1888, the National Geographic Society has funded more than 14,000 research, conservation, education, and storytelling projects around the world. National Geographic Partners distributes a portion of the funds it receives from your purchase to National Geographic Society to support programs including the conservation of animals and their habitats. To learn more, visit natgeo.com/info.

For more information, visit nationalgeographic.com, call 1-877-873-6846, or write to the following address:
National Geographic Partners, LLC
1145 17th Street NW
Washington, DC 20036-4688 U.S.A.

More for kids from National Geographic: natgeokids.com

For rights or permissions inquiries, please contact National Geographic Books Subsidiary Rights: bookrights@natgeo.com

Series design by 3+Co. and Jim Hiscott.
The body text in the book is set in Mrs. Eaves.
The display text is Lisboa.

The Library of Congress cataloged the 2007 edition as follows:

Heiligman, Deborah.
 Celebrate Rosh Hashanah and Yom Kippur / Deborah Heiligman ; consultant, Shira Stern.
     p. cm. — (Holidays around the world)
 Includes bibliographical references and index.
 ISBN 978-1-4263-0076-9 (trade : alk. paper)
 ISBN 978-1-4263-0077-6 (library : alk. paper)
 1. High Holidays—Juvenile literature. I. Title.
BM693.H5H45 2007
296.4'31—dc22

                              2006100317

2016 paperback edition ISBN: 978-1-4263-2628-8
2016 reinforced library binding edition ISBN: 978-1-4263-2629-5

Printed in Canada
23/FC/2

ACKNOWLEDGMENTS

Thanks to Brad Hoffman who brought his camera to brunch and spent most of his time taking photographs of the honey cake I made. Thanks to the Cornfeld family: to Janet and Sarah for orchestrating the shoot, to Michael for orchestrating them; to Jennifer for Brad and to Melissa for the chocolates. Thanks to Marfé Ferguson Delano for shepherding this book so expertly from beginning to end and to Lori Epstein for finding photographs where none existed. Thanks to Rabbi Sandy Roth and Kehilat HaNahar for all those years of beautiful Rosh Hashanah and Yom Kippur services. Thanks to Julie Stockler. And most of all, thanks to Rabbi Shira Stern for the honey cake recipe (it's the best I've ever tasted!), for her great counsel, and for her friendship. It's not the last one, Shira, I promise.